The World's Best Marriage Jokes

In this series:

The World's Best Dirty Jokes
More of the World's Best Dirty Jokes
Still More of the World's Best Dirty Jokes
The World's Best Irish Jokes
More of the World's Best Irish Jokes
Still More of the World's Best Irish Jokes
The World's Best Jewish Jokes
More of the World's Best Jewish Jokes
More of the World's Best Doctor Jokes
The World's Best Dirty Stories
The World's Best Dirty Limericks
The Word's Best Dirty Songs
The World's Best Business Jokes
The World's Best Mother-in-Law Jokes
The World's Best Fishing Jokes
The World's Best Salesman Jokes
The World's Best Doctor Jokes
The World's Best Golf Jokes
More of the World's Best Golf Jokes
The World's Best Scottish Jokes
The World's Best Football Jokes
The World's Best Cricket Jokes
The World's Best Lawyer Jokes
The World's Best Holiday Jokes
The World's Best Acting Jokes
The World's Best Drinking Jokes
More of the World's Best Drinking Jokes
The World's Best Gardening Jokes
The World's Best Motoring Jokes
The World's Best After-Dinner Jokes
The World's Best Skiing Jokes
The World's Best Boss Jokes

The World's Best Marriage Jokes

Ernest Forbes

Illustrated by Graham Morris

HarperCollinsPublishers

HarperCollins*Publishers*,
77–85 Fulham Palace Road,
Hammersmith, London W6 8JB

This paperback edition 1993
3 5 7 9 8 6 4 2

First published in Great Britain by
Fontana 1992

A catalogue record for this book
is available from the British Library

ISBN 0 00 637839 0

Set in Goudy Old Style

Printed in Great Britain by
HarperCollinsManufacturing Glasgow

It was a very warm day and the husband announced he was going to sunbathe in the back garden.

'I wonder what the neighbours would say if I sunbathed in the nude,' he remarked.

'They would probably say I married you for your money,' replied his wife.

The two men had been introduced at a party and were sitting in silence, amid the noise of the celebrations, sipping their drinks.

'You may have noticed I'm a man of few words,' remarked one, suddenly.

'Yes, I'm married too,' the other man quietly replied.

Two days before his wedding the prospective bridegroom was struck by a cricket ball in a very vulnerable spot. He went to a doctor who said cheerfully,

'Sorry, old boy, I'll have to put it in splints.'

On their wedding night the couple went to their bedroom and the bride undressed. Standing naked she indicated her breasts and said, 'Aren't they beautiful? Never been touched by any other hand!'

The bridegroom removed his trousers and smiled. 'Look at this,' he said, 'it hasn't even been unpacked!'

He was a man who had an inflated opinion of himself. At a party one night he was explaining how smart he had been in life.

'Even in my marriage I was a winner, I married a very clever woman,' he boasted. 'My wife can talk for hours on any subject.'

'Really?' said a bored listener. 'My wife doesn't need a subject.'

'Do you know,' complained one wife, 'my husband is so lazy he could sit and watch the grass grow.'

'That's nothing,' snorted another wife. 'I saw a snail on the step yesterday as we came in and I gave my husband a nudge and told him to get rid of it. When I asked him if he had killed it he said, "No, it got away!"'

'This is my religious suit,' explained a man to his office colleague.

'What do you mean, your religious suit?' asked the colleague.

'Well, every time I put it on my wife says, "Oh God!"'

'You never cry out when you have an orgasm,' complained her husband.

'You're never with me when I have an orgasm,' replied his wife.

The married couple always went on holiday together so the husband was surprised and annoyed when his wife, who claimed she was feeling 'run down', announced she was going to Spain for two weeks with her friend Sally.

Towards the end of the holiday the wife faxed her husband. 'Am feeling a new woman. Mind if I stay another week?'

She received a speedy reply from her husband: 'So am I. Stay two!'

Ken Green typified the henpecked husband: small, mild mannered and meek. The only bright spot of his year was the annual dinner with former class mates. At one dinner, a prize was awarded to the man who told the most amusing story of making love to his wife. Ken won the prize with his story and was awarded a vase.

Highly elated, he carried his prize home only to be confronted by his wife who demanded: 'What is that?'

'Er . . . er . . . it's a prize, dear,' stuttered Ken.

'A prize for what?' questioned his wife.

'For tell . . . for tell . . . for telling them about a personal experience,' stammered a pale Ken, suddenly aware he couldn't tell his wife the truth.

'What did you tell them about?' demanded the woman.

'About the time I played pitch and putt at the holiday camp,' gurgled her husband.

'Hmm,' grunted the wife and walked away.

The following day Mrs Green met the wife of a man who had attended the dinner.

'Hello, Mrs Green,' greeted the woman, 'my husband tells me your husband won the prize for the best story at the dinner last night.'

'I don't know why,' replied Mrs Green. 'He only did it once and his cap blew off, he couldn't get it in the hole and he lost a ball!'

Two husbands were earnestly discussing marriage. 'You know I never knew the meaning of happiness until I got married,' observed one.

'Yes,' replied the second man sadly, 'and then it's too late.'

The husband returned from work on a very hot day and went to the refrigerator to get a cold drink. He was very surprised to find his wife sitting in the fridge. 'What are you doing in there?' he gasped.

'Well,' replied his wife coyly, 'it's such a very hot day, I thought you'd like to slip into something cool when you came home.'

'I believe your husband was injured watching a football match on Saturday,' remarked Mrs Jones.

'Yes,' replied Mrs Brown, 'the old fool was so drunk he tried to surf on the Mexican wave.'

The elderly married couple, both octogenarians, shuffled into the doctor's surgery and eventually got seated comfortably.

'It's my leg, doctor,' said the husband. 'I've pains in my leg.'

'Yes, doctor,' confirmed the wife. 'It's his leg. He's got pains in his leg.'

'This leg?' asked the doctor, tapping the man's right leg.

'No, the other one,' grunted the man.

'No, the other one,' echoed his wife.

'Did you injure it?' enquired the doctor as he examined the offending limb.

'No, I didn't. Just have pains in it,' replied the man.

'No, he didn't. He just has pains in it,' agreed the wife.

'Well,' said the doctor when he had completed his examination, 'I have to tell you it's just old age.'

'But, doctor, how can that be?' interjected the wife. 'His other leg is just as old and there's not a thing wrong with it.'

It had not been a happy marriage but for forty nagging, bickering years they had been together. One day, the wife stepped in front of a bus which didn't stop and the lady passed to her great reward in heaven.

After the funeral, the husband returned to his bungalow and, as he inserted the key in the lock of the front door, a roof tile slipped and hit him on the head. As he lay on the ground rubbing the injured part, he looked to the sky and cried: 'Christ! Are you up there already!'

To celebrate their parents' silver wedding anniversary the children arranged a surprise party. During the festivities the drink flowed freely and, eventually, the children called upon their father for a speech on twenty-five happy years.

The husband struggled to his feet and swayed as he raised his glass. 'Yes,' he said, 'I had twenty-five wonderful years of happiness – then I married your mother!'

Marriage is an old institution – but, then, who wants to live in an old institution?

A doctor was giving a talk on safer sex to married couples of all ages and requested members of the group to join in by answering the questions he would put to them. His first question was for a show of hands of those present who had sex more than once a week. After this he increased the length of time but, after several questions, the doctor noticed that a little man sitting in the front row never raised his hand although he had indicated he was married to a lady of ample figure sitting beside him.

The doctor pondered for a moment then asked. 'Is there anyone who has sex only once a year?'

The little man in the front row waved his hand vigorously. 'I do! I do! I do!' he shouted with gusto.

'Only once a year?' enquired the doctor.

'Yes,' replied the little man cheerfully.

'You seem to be quite happy about it,' said the doctor.

'Well, tonight's the night!' exclaimed the little man.

At a party, a wife remarked proudly to the hostess. 'My husband dresses so well.'

'Yes,' cooed the hostess, 'and so quickly.'

'I blame myself for the tragic death of my husband,' confided May.

'Whatever makes you say that?' questioned Rosemary.

'I shot him,' replied May.

'My husband is so evasive that when I asked him his favourite colour he said, "plaid".'

The Ladies' Guild decided to help the Save the Children Fund by having a white elephant stall at the local fete. The members of the guild and their friends were invited to contribute to the effort by bringing along to the stall something they didn't want.

Fourteen women brought their husbands.

'That's very interesting,' said a husband to his wife as he glanced up from the newspaper he was reading. 'The Jews have named a holiday after your sex life.'

'Oh,' said the wife icily, 'what is it?'

'Passover.'

'If the Chancellor of the Exchequer can't balance his budget,' pointed out the wife, 'why do you expect me to balance ours?'

'Mrs Jones,' said the doctor, 'you're overtired because of too much sex. How often do you have sexual intercourse?'

'Monday, Tuesday, Thursday, Saturday and Sunday,' replied Mrs Jones.

'Well, cut out Sunday night,' said the doctor.

'I can't do that,' answered Mrs Jones. 'That's the night I'm with my husband.'

Elizabeth Ann watched as her husband carefully made his selection of eight draws on the football coupon. 'What do you hope to win?' she asked.

'Two million pounds,' came the reply, with great feeling.

'What about the begging letters?' enquired his wife.

'Oh, we'll keep sending them,' replied her husband.

John and Jane had been married fifty years and Jane said in a loving voice. 'You know John, we've been married fifty years and I've been by your side for all that time.'

'Indeed you have Jane, indeed you have,' replied John. 'When I was wounded in World War II you were by my side to nurse me back to health, so I could go back to battle and get wounded again and, then, once more, you were by my side. Then, after the war, when I couldn't get a job you were by my side. Eventually, I got a job and had to work twelve hours a day to make ends meet and, again, you were by my side. We didn't go on holidays so we could buy our own little home and you were there, by my side. The time I had eight draws correct on the football coupon but you had forgotten to post it you were still there by my side. During the Thatcher years I was made redundant and we lost our little home, our car and our savings but you were there, by my side. We're living in two rooms now and I'm too old to get another job but you're still by my side. All in all, Jane, you're a bloody jinx!'

The married woman was having her house painted and, when she got up one morning, noticed a hand print on the door frame.

She called downstairs to the painter. 'Would you like to come up here a minute? I'd like to show you where my husband put his hand last night.'

'If it's all the same to you, missus,' replied the painter, 'I'll settle for a cup of tea.'

A man entered a police station and approached the desk sergeant. 'I want to report that my wife is missing,' he said as he handed over a photograph. 'That is my wife and I want her found immediately.'

The desk sergeant studied the photograph for a minute, then asked, 'Why?'

As they returned from a party the wife said, 'Do you realize what you did?'

'No,' replied the husband, 'but I'll admit I was wrong. What did I do?'

The newlyweds walked into the lobby of the hotel and a beautiful, well-built blonde looked at them in surprise and said. 'Hello, Ted, darling, what are you doing here?'

Ted made a lighthearted reply and moved quickly to the lift. Once inside the lift, the bride demanded. 'Who was that woman?'

'Oh, Christ!' exclaimed Ted. 'Don't you start, I'm going to have enough trouble explaining you to her!'

Arriving home unexpectedly from a business trip, the husband found his wife in bed with a strange man. 'What the hell do you two think you're doing?'

'See,' said the wife, nudging the man beside her. 'Didn't I tell you he was stupid?'

'Do you think my salary will be sufficient to keep you, darling?' asked the bridegroom.

'Oh, I'll try and make it do,' replied the bride. 'But what about you?'

A man stood in front of a mirror looking at himself admiringly while he groomed his hair and adjusted his gold neckchain.

'I wonder how many charming and attractive men there are in this world,' he said to his wife.

'One less than you think,' she answered.

Mr Jones was sitting behind the newspaper having his breakfast. After eating and reading for about twenty minutes, he lowered the newspaper and asked his wife. 'Did you say something dear?'

'No, that was yesterday,' replied his wife.

While dancing with her husband, the wife's brooch became unfastened and slid down the back of her gown. Not wanting to cause any fuss, she asked her husband to try and retrieve it. He slid his hand down the back of her gown and after a cautious search said, 'I can't find it.'

'A little lower,' said his wife.

The husband tried a little lower without success.

'Still lower,' whispered his wife.

Suddenly aware that some dancers were watching him, the husband muttered, 'I feel a proper ass.'

'Never mind that,' snapped his wife. 'Just get the bloody brooch!'

The husband had taken his wife to a rugby match and had shouted himself hoarse in support of his team. After the match, he croaked, 'You'll have to excuse me, darling, but I've lost my voice.'

'That's all right, dear,' replied his wife, 'you'll find it in my right ear!'

A sharp knock on the hotel door startled the two lovers.

'Quick, it's my husband,' cried the frightened woman. 'Jump out the window!'

'But we're on the thirteenth floor,' her lover gasped.

'Jump!' ordered the woman. 'This is no time to be superstitious.'

The two wives were having their morning coffee and the conversation was about men.

'It's not fair,' said Judy, 'men can look at us and tell how well we're equipped physically, but we can't tell how well a man is equipped unless we go to bed with him.'

'Of course we can,' replied Jane. 'Look at the size of his feet.'

'His feet?'

'Yes. The bigger his feet the bigger his you-know-what.'

'I didn't know that,' said an interested Judy.

'What size of shoes does your husband wear?'

'Size nine.'

'Well, go to bed with a man who wears a different size and you can make the comparison,' suggested Jane.

'That would be cheating. Just like having an affair,' pointed out Judy.

'Not really,' said the ever helpful Jane. 'Put it down to research.'

Judy was still thinking of Jane's proposal when, a couple of days later, a young electrician called at the house to carry out some work.

Judy looked at him thoughtfully and asked. 'What size shoes do you wear?'

'Why do you ask?' laughed the young man.

'Well, my husband got a new pair of shoes which he doesn't like and I thought they might fit you,' answered Judy.

'I wear size ten,' came the reply.

'Too bad. Wrong size.'

After the electrician had finished his work, he found himself in bed with Judy. As he prepared to leave the house Judy handed him some money.

'Don't be silly,' exclaimed the young man. 'I wanted to go to bed with you.'

'Oh, it's not for going to bed with me,' explained Judy. 'It's to get you a new pair of shoes, the ones you're wearing are too small and must be killing you!'

Returning from the funeral of his beautiful wife the widower was deeply grieved.

'I know how sad you are,' the minister said, 'but you are young and, in time, this wound will heal. You will meet someone with whom you will be very happy.'

'I know, I know,' said the widower, 'but what about *tonight*?'

'Good morning, Mrs Hooper,' greeted Dr Parker as the woman entered his surgery. 'Please be seated and tell me how you are feeling.'

'I feel fine, Dr Parker,' replied the woman. 'It's my husband I'm worried about and, as he came to see you two weeks ago, I thought you would tell me what he's suffering from. His behaviour is very strange.'

'Yes,' said the doctor. 'Your husband was with me recently and I prescribed some treatment. Has he not told you about his problem?'

'No, he has not,' retorted Mrs Hooper. 'When I ask him he just grunts and walks away. He's always scratching his elbow and moaning softly. I thought, perhaps, he was suffering from some nervous condition.'

'Nothing of the sort,' said the doctor. 'He has haemorrhoids.'

'Haemorrhoids!' exclaimed Mrs Hooper. 'But why does he keep scratching his elbow?'

'Well, you should know Mrs Hooper. Your husband is a civil servant and as a civil servant he doesn't know his arse from his elbow!'

'What makes you think you have a perfect husband?'
'Well, he remembers my birthday but forgets my age.'

A husband and wife both had black hair but when their first child, a daughter, was born she was a redhead. This upset the father so much he consulted his doctor.

'Look, doctor, there has never been a redhead in either my family or my wife's, so why should my daughter have red hair?'

'How long have you been married?' asked the doctor.

'Ten years.'

'How often do you and your wife have sex?'

'Two or three times a year,' replied the man.

'That explains it,' said the doctor. 'You're rusty.'

Betty awoke one night screaming with pain, so Bob telephoned the doctor.

'Come quickly,' Bob told the doctor, 'my wife Betty is in great pain. I think it's her appendix.'

'Go back to bed,' the doctor told him. 'I took your wife's

appendix out three years ago and I've never heard of anyone having another appendix!'

'Ever heard of anyone having another wife?' asked Bob.

I t was the first night of the honeymoon and the newlyweds were snuggling in bed.

'Darling,' said the bride, 'will you love me always?'

'Of course, my sweet,' replied the groom. 'Which way would you like me to try first?'

O ne good thing about a nudist wedding: you never have to ask who the best man is.

'Y ou have the most beautiful houseplants,' said Linda. 'How do you do it?'

'Well, you know they recommend you talk to your plants? It so happens I talk to my husband – he doesn't listen but the plants do,' replied Vera.

T he wife telephoned her solicitor and exclaimed. 'I want a divorce.'

'On what grounds?' asked the solicitor.

'Oh, I've got the grounds.'

'Well, what are they?'

'My husband says I'm rotten in bed,' shouted the wife.

'So?' said the solicitor.

'How does he know the difference?'

A Member of Parliament had just returned after a trip abroad. On his first night home, he was in bed with his wife when there was a great flash of lightning which lit up the room. To the astonishment of his wife he jumped out of bed shouting, 'I'll buy the negative! I'll buy the negative!'

A woman was reading an item from a newspaper and said to her husband. 'Listen to this, dear, there's a report here of a man who said he would swop his wife for tickets for the test match at Lords. You wouldn't do anything like that, would you, dear?'

'No, of course not,' snorted her husband. 'I've already got tickets!'

The husband broke open a fortune cookie and started to laugh. His wife immediately grabbed the cookie and said, 'Hmm. So you're going to have a beautiful and charming wife, are you? Not while I'm alive, Philip, not while I'm alive.'

'I've just heard the strangest thing,' observed the husband to his wife. 'It appears our milkman claims he has slept with every woman in this street except one. Can you believe that?'

'Oh, I believe it,' replied his wife sharply, her eyes glinting. 'I bet it's that stuck-up cow in number four.'

An Irishman approached his minister and said he wanted to get married again. The minister told him he could only have one wife and the man was surprised.

'That's not what you told me the last time,' the man responded. 'You said for better, for worse, for richer, for poorer and that's sixteen.'

You told me before we were married that you were well-off,' complained the wife.

'Yes, I know, but I didn't know how well-off I was!' replied the husband.

Husbands are like fish: neither would get into trouble if they kept their mouths shut.

'I can always tell when my husband is lying,' remarked a wife.

'How can you tell?' asked a friend.

'His lips move.'

'Darling,' she whispered, 'will you still love me after we are married?'

'Probably even more,' he replied. 'I've always had a weakness for married women.'

The two office workers were complaining about the short lunch break.

'The boss takes an hour and a half every day and expects us to get by on thirty minutes,' muttered Dick.

'If I had an extra fifteen minutes I could go home for lunch,' Jim pointed out.

'The boss is never around at noon so why don't you take the extra time?' suggested Dick.

Jim agreed and that very day went home for lunch. His wife wasn't expecting him so, when he didn't find her downstairs, he looked in the bedroom. When he opened the door, he saw his wife in bed with his boss. Jim slipped out of the house quietly and back to the office.

The following morning, Dick asked him if he was going to take the extra fifteen minutes again that day.

'Hell, no,' retorted Jim. 'I almost got caught yesterday.'

'I'm sorry to tell you, Mrs O'Reilly, that your husband will never be able to work again,' advised the doctor.

'Oh, thanks, doctor,' replied Mrs O'Reilly. 'I'll just go and tell him, that'll cheer him up no end!'

'Victor asked me to marry him and make him the happiest man in the world,' declared Iris.

'And which did you decide to do?' questioned Margaret.

Arthur went to his local pub every night leaving his wife, Iris, to look after the three children. His nightly outings

annoyed his wife, particularly as when he left he would shout, 'Cheerio, mother of three.'

One night, Iris was in every bad form and in reply to Arthur's 'Cheerio, mother of three' she called back, 'Cheerio, father of one.'

'My husband is so stupid he thinks a bigamist is an Italian fog.'

'You know,' confided one wife, 'I had my husband well insured.'

'What did you get out of it?' asked the other wife.

'My second husband.'

The man had a row with his mistress and returned home early only to find his wife in bed with another man.

'What's the meaning of this?' he demanded. 'Who is this man?'

'That's a fair question,' replied the wife as she rolled over. 'What *is* your name?'

The woman was hurrying along the street when she was stopped by her friend, Susan.

'What's the hurry?' asked Susan.

'I'm rushing to the doctor. I don't like the look of my husband.'

'I'll come too, I hate the sight of mine!'

The husband came home from the office, threw his briefcase down and exclaimed. 'What a time! I'm not myself today!'

'Good,' answered his wife. 'I thought I noticed an improvement.'

A woman was telling her friend about the sudden death of her husband.

'What happened?' asked the friend.

'He went out to the back garden to pick some peas for the dinner and just dropped dead.'

'That's terrible. What did you do?'

'Well, I had to open a tin of beans instead.'

A man got out of a car at a farmhouse and spoke to the woman standing in the doorway. 'Are you Mrs Sullivan?'

'That I am,' declared the woman.

'I want to speak to your husband.'

'He's working in the pig sty.'

'May I go and see him?'

'Certainly. You'll easily know him, he'll be smoking a pipe.'

'Do you mean to tell me a physical wreck like your husband was able to hit you?' enquired the surprised police officer.

'Ah, but officer,' replied the extremely large woman, 'he wasn't a physical wreck before he hit me!'

'My husband and I fought for twenty-five years before it came to an end,' said Mrs Smithers.
'Then did you bury the hatchet?' asked Mrs Spencer.
'No, my husband.'

'I'm not saying Margaret's husband is mean, but when he goes to a fancy dress party he always goes as Napoleon so he can keep one hand on his wallet.'

Susan: 'How is your husband doing with that new diet?'
Sheila: 'Wonderful. He disappeared last week.'

'Darling, I have a confession to make,' said the shy young bride as they enjoyed their first breakfast together. 'It isn't a big thing but perhaps I should have told you before – sometimes I suffer from asthma.'
'Thank God,' said the smiling groom. 'Last night, I thought you were hissing me.'

A sign displayed in the lounge of a private house: 'The views expressed by my husband are not necessarily those of the management.'

The woman walked into a legal office and requested advice.
'What is your problem?' enquired the lawyer.
'I want to divorce my husband,' explained the woman.
'On what grounds?'

'Infidelity,' replied the woman. 'I don't think my husband has been faithful to me.'

'What makes you think that?' probed the lawyer.

'Well,' said the woman. 'I don't think he's the father of my daughter.'

'A penny for your thoughts,' said a husband to his wife. 'You better make it £45,' answered the wife. 'I'm thinking of buying a new hat.'

'They say your ex-wife has made up her mind to marry a struggling young writer,' remarked John.

'Well, if she has made up her mind he might as well stop struggling,' commented David.

As a wife, Margaret was not a gift from Heaven. She was stubborn, unpleasant, domineering, selfish, uncaring, loud, thoughtless and boring. She believed in the old-fashioned values – providing they suited her; claimed she never told a lie in her life – only changed her mind; had a habit of wearing blue and swinging her handbag.

Her husband was different – affable, good company and liked a cigarette and a drink. So, on his birthday when his wife gave him a gift of two ties, he immediately knotted one in position to show his appreciation.

'Well, what do you think?' he asked.

'What's wrong with the other one?' demanded Margaret.

He was ninety-two years old and married a girl of eighteen. As they prepared for bed on their wedding night he asked her, 'Did your mother tell you the facts of life?'

'No,' replied the girl quietly and blushed.

'That's too bad,' muttered the man. 'Because I'm afraid I've forgotten them.'

A man with six children was getting deeper in debt and found it difficult to support the large family. One day, in despair, he cried to his wife, 'If you ever get pregnant again I'll kill myself.'

A few months later, his wife greeted him with the news that she was going to have a baby.

The husband ran upstairs to the bedroom, pulled his shotgun out of the wardrobe, loaded it and placed it at his head.

'Stop! Stop!' yelled his wife. 'You're killing an innocent man!'

Wife: 'When I married you I thought you were a brave man.'
Husband: 'So did all my friends.'

Mrs Stewart was almost in tears. 'Oh, Sally,' she said to her hair stylist, 'I believe my husband is having an affair with his secretary.'

'I don't believe you,' snapped Sally. 'You're only saying that to make me jealous.'

'That wife of mine is a liar,' said an angry Sammy to his pal as they sat drinking in the pub.

'How do you know?' his friend asked.

'She didn't come home last night and when I asked where she had been, she said she spent the night with her sister Barbara.'

'Well, what's wrong with that?'

'She's a liar. Because I spent the night with her sister Barbara.'

The man and his wife were discussing the husband's business partner as they were having a drink. 'Do you trust your partner?' asked the wife.

'Trust him?' cried her husband. 'Why I'd trust him with my life.'

'Yes, I know that, but would you trust him with anything of value?' questioned the wife.

When a man and a woman marry they become one, but the question is – which one?

They made mad, passionate love, then he lit two cigarettes, passing one to the girl.

'I really love having sex with you,' he said, 'but marriage is out of the question. I love you like a sister.'

'Christ!' exclaimed the girl. 'What a home life you must have had!'

The divorce court listened as the wealthy woman stated to the judge that her husband left her bed and board. At this point, the husband rose and said: 'I must correct that statement, sir. I left her bed – *bored!*'

The widow was grief stricken on the death of her husband and had inscribed on his headstone:
'The light of my life has gone out.'
When she remarried a few months later she got the stonemason to add the word 'temporarily'.

'You know I said something to my wife about a week ago and she hasn't spoken to me since,' remarked Des.
'I wish you could remember what you said and I'll try it,' declared John.

'What are you nagging me about?' complained the husband. 'I was in last night by a quarter of twelve.'
'You were not, so don't lie to me,' screamed his wife. 'I heard you come in and the clock was striking three.'
'Well,' shouted the husband, 'isn't three a quarter of twelve?'

'My husband never worked a day when he was alive but I'm glad to say he's working hard now,' said Mrs Green.
'Whatever do you mean?' asked her friend.
'Well, I had him cremated and put his ashes in an egg-timer,' replied Mrs Green.

J ack and Don were having a drink in their local when Don confessed that all was not well at home.

'My wife and I don't seem to hit it off at night,' moaned Don. 'I hate to admit it, but I'm afraid I just don't know how to make her happy.'

'Dammit, Don,' said Jack. 'There's really nothing to it. Let me give you some advice. Before you go to bed have a nightcap to help you relax then, in the bedroom, put on some music – something soft and romantic – dim the lights. Tell your wife to wear her sheerest nightie and make sure you leave the window open.'

'Then what do I do?' asked Don.

'Just whistle.'

'Whistle?'

'That's right. I'll be waiting outside the window. When I hear you whistle, I'll come right in and finish the job.'

O ver drinks the two men were in an argument about the charms of a popular film actress.

'I say she's overrated,' said one. 'Take away her large eyes, her beautiful hair, her wonderful figure and what have you got?'

'My wife,' said the other man with a heavy sigh.

T he husband and wife, both suffering from hangovers, sipped their morning coffee in silence.

'Tell me, darling,' whispered the husband holding his head. 'At the party last night was it you I made love to on the stairs?'

His wife looked at him reflectively, and then asked, 'About what time?'

'I am the happiest girl in the world. I am going to marry the man I want,' cried Susan.

'Balls!' snapped Ruth. 'Real happiness comes to a girl by marrying a man someone else wants.'

'If you don't marry me,' said Roger to Donna in desperation, 'I'll hang myself on the tree in your front garden.'

'Don't do that, for goodness sake,' said Donna. 'You know my parents don't like you hanging about the house.'

'I wouldn't marry you if you were the last man on earth. You are stupid, repulsive, mean and utterly miserable. In fact, I hate you,' cried Joan.

'Is that a yes or no?' queried Mick.

The expectant father paced the waiting room in the maternity wing.

'This is our first child,' he said to the old-hand who was sitting in an armchair trying to pick winners for the horse racing. 'Have you any children?'

'Seven,' replied the old-hand, lowering his racing guide.

'Seven?' said the man sitting near the old-hand. 'Tell me,

how long . . . er, how long . . . er . . . is it before you can have sex with your wife after the birth?'

'Well, that depends,' answered the old-hand, 'on whether she's in a ward or a private room.'

Marriage starts with billing and cooing, but only the billing lasts.

The husband arrived home unexpectedly and saw a cigar smouldering in the ashtray. 'Where did that come from?' he thundered at his trembling wife.

There was a pregnant pause, then from the wardrobe a meek male voice squeaked, 'Cuba!'

There are two periods in a man's life when he never understands women – before he is married and afterwards.

Helen had been named as co-respondent in a divorce case, and was being questioned in court.

'So, Miss Graham, you admit you stayed in a hotel with this man?'

'Yes, I do, but I couldn't help it,' answered the girl.

'Couldn't help it? Why not?'

'He deceived me.'

'And how did he do that?'

'Well,' replied Helen earnestly, 'he told the hotel receptionist that I was his wife.'

Slipping into his house, the husband caught his wife in bed with a naked man. Producing a gun from his pocket, he was going to shoot the man when his wife pleaded:

'Please don't shoot him! Please don't shoot him! Who do you think bought us the cottage by the sea and our new car? Who do you think paid for our holiday to Australia?'

'Did you pay for all that?' demanded the husband.

The naked man nodded.

'Then get your clothes on,' roared the husband. 'Do you want to catch cold?'

'Have you ever thought what you would do if you had the Queen's income?' asked the husband.

'No, but I've often wondered what she would do if she had mine,' replied the wife.

'Hello, Peter. How's your wife?'
'Compared to what?'

They sat looking at her engagement ring. 'Did your friends admire it?' her fiancé enquired.

'They did more than that,' she replied. 'Three of them recognized it.'

A man got a gravestone for his wife while she was still alive. On it he had the stonemason carve:

'Here lies my wife; cold as usual'.

His wife was very angry so she got him a gravestone with the inscription:

'Here lies my husband; stiff at last'.

Mr Mills came home one day to find his wife in bed with his neighbour, Mr Adams. Very upset, Mr Mills dashed next door calling, 'Mrs Adams, your husband's in bed with my wife.'

Mrs Adams calmed him down.

'Look, don't take it so hard. Sit down and we'll have a cup of tea and talk about it.'

Mr Mills drank his tea and felt much calmer. 'What should we do about this affair?'

'Let's have a little revenge,' suggested Mrs Adams.

They lay down on the couch and made love, after which Mr Mills drank another cup of tea. They had more revenge and more tea and Mrs Adams suggested some more revenge.

'Look,' said Mr Mills, 'I have no hard feelings left.'

A man rushed into a police station and said he wanted to give himself up because he had assaulted his wife with a cricket bat.

'Did you kill her?' asked the police officer.

'No,' gasped the man. 'That's why I'm here!'

A Member of Parliament arrived home from work unexpectantly and found his wife in bed with his best friend, Cecil. 'Why you, Cecil?' he cried. 'I have to. But why you?'

A man came home from work tired and very despondent and grumbled to his wife: 'I was late for work today.'
'I know,' answered his wife.
'I had a fight with the boss.'
'I know,' she replied.
'He sacked me,' moaned the husband.
'I know,' nodded the wife.'
'How the hell do you know?' the husband asked angrily.
'He told me,' smiled the wife.
'Told you? Well, screw him!' shouted the husband.
'I did,' said the wife. 'You go back to work on Monday.'

A woman returned from the doctor's and said to her husband. 'Dr Hill says I'm in good shape and he even admired my breasts.'
'Did he,' enquired the husband, 'say anything about your big fat ass?'
'No. He never mentioned your name,' replied the wife.

A father of four came home carrying a bag of sweets and lined up his children.
'Now, kids,' he said. 'The person who never talks back to Mother, always listens to her and does what he or she is told will get the sweets. Who is it to be?'
There was silence for a moment and then a chorus of voices replied: 'You get them, Daddy!'

A London businessman went to Paris to buy stock for a fashion house and his wife was very disappointed when he told her she could not accompany him. He was to be away

a week but, at the end of the week, he telephoned her to say he would have to stay another week as he was still buying. At the end of the second week, he again telephoned to say he would have to remain there as he was still buying.

'If you stay there another week, darling,' said his wife, 'I'll start selling what you are buying.'

A beautiful blonde was standing at the arrival lounge of the airport waiting for her husband. When she spotted him at the customs counter, she waved a welcome. Her husband saw her, waved back and shouted, 'F. F.'

His wife replied by shouting, 'E. F.'

They exchanged 'F. F.' and 'E. F.' a couple of times and then the customs officer said to the husband. 'Is that some sort of a code you have with that lady?'

'Oh, that's my wife,' replied the man, 'and she's just saying she wants to eat first.'

C harles was taking evening classes at the Adult Further Education Centre and was critical of his friend Ted for not doing the same.

'It's amazing what you learn,' said Charles. 'For instance, who is Dan Quayle?'

'I don't know,' answered Ted.

'He's the Vice President of the United States of America,' informed Charles. 'Do you know who Mary Robinson is?'

'No,' admitted Ted.

'She's the President of Ireland,' replied Charles. 'You see, you should go to night school.'

'May I ask you a question?' queried Ted.

'Certainly.'

'Do you know who Freddie Simpson is?' asked Ted.

'No, I don't,' acknowledged Charles. 'Who is he?'

'He's the fellow who visits your wife every night when you're at evening classes,' smiled Ted.

T he couple on their honeymoon went for a country walk. As they walked down a quiet lane the husband became very amorous and suggested they climb over a wall, get into a field and make love.

'How am I going to get over the wall?' asked the bride.

'You could stand on this,' said the husband, indicating signs of his desire.

'Oh, sure, that's fine,' replied the girl. 'But how am I supposed to get back?'

F red was engaged to a very beautiful young blonde girl who had an identical twin sister. They dressed alike, walked alike, talked alike and had the same mannerisms.

'Tell me, Fred,' said Larry. 'Do you not find it very difficult to distinguish one from the other?'

'Frankly,' replied Fred, 'I don't try.'

The minister called in on a bible study group for juniors and patted a few heads. 'Tell me,' he asked little Tommy, 'what do you know about matrimony?'

'Sir, matrimony is a place of great suffering and sorrow,' replied little Tommy.

'No, no, Tommy,' said the teacher. 'You're describing purgatory.'

'Leave the little fellow alone,' counselled the minister. 'He may well be right!'

Denis died and went to hell. Within a month the Spirit of Evil sent for him and said, 'Since you arrived here you've done nothing but cause trouble. In fact, the way you act you'd think you owned the place.'

'Well, why shouldn't I act like that?' demanded Denis. 'Margaret gave it to me before I died.'

The telephone rang in the ambulance control room and an excited male caller yelled, 'Send an ambulance quickly, my wife Lynn is about to have a baby!'

'Tell me, sir,' said the control operator calmly, 'is this her first baby?'

'No,' replied the caller, 'this is her husband Mark speaking.'

Paul was standing at the window looking out when he said, 'Oh look, there's the woman Jack Bennet is in love with.'

His wife jumped from a chair, knocked over a table and

pushed past him to have a look. 'Paul, you fool, that's his wife.'

'I know,' said Paul with a smile.

I t was a very sweet marriage proposal but Sally refused the offer.

'Why will you not marry me?' asked Dirk.

'Well, if you must know, I'm a lesbian,' replied Sally.

'But that's no problem,' argued Dirk. 'You can go to your church and I'll go to mine.'

I t was the first night of their honeymoon and Carol put on her new short sexy nightie and slipped into bed. She waited for her husband who did not appear so, eventually, she got out of bed and found him standing on the bedroom balcony looking at the stars.

'Why don't you come to bed?' Carol asked.

'My mother told me that this would be the most exciting night of my life,' replied Mark. 'I don't want to miss any of it by going to bed.'

'I think my husband is ashamed of me,' said Mrs Dunn.

'What makes you say that?' asked Mrs Roberts.

'Well, the other night, I asked him if we had sexual relations and he said we had. Yet, in the ten years we've been married, he's never introduced me to any of them,' replied Mrs Dunn.

After a courtship of twenty years, Janet decided to bring matters to a head. 'Angus,' she said, 'do you not think it's about time we were getting married?'

'Woman, dear,' replied Angus, puffing at his pipe, 'who would marry either of us at this stage of our lives?'

'George, George, come quickly!' yelled the wife. 'Mother is being attacked by a mad dog!'

'Why should I care what happens to a mad dog?' shouted her husband.

When a couple got married they decided not to refer to any extramarital affairs they might have until they reached their silver wedding anniversary. They both agreed to keep a jar into which they would drop a grain of rice any time they were unfaithful.

After twenty-five years the wife opened the husband's jar and found seven grains of rice.

'Oh,' she exclaimed, 'what a wonderful husband you have been to me. Unfaithful only seven times.'

The husband opened the wife's jar and saw only one grain of rice. Very pleased, he hugged and kissed his wife. 'How come there is only one grain in your jar?'

'Don't you remember, dear,' replied the wife, 'I made you a rice pudding for dessert last night?'

A man went to an unisex salon for a trim and manicure. Seated comfortably in the chair he said to the pretty manicurist. 'How about having a drink with me tonight?'

'I can't,' replied the girl. 'I'm married.'

'Tell your husband you have to work late,' suggested the customer.

'You tell him,' said the manicurist. 'He's cutting your hair.'

Tommy was sitting on his father's knee listening to a fairy story. 'Daddy, do all fairy stories start with "Once upon a time"?'

'No,' cut in his mother quickly. 'A lot of them start with "Darling, I have to work late at the office tonight . . ."'

Jane: 'Would you marry a man who was your inferior?'
Joan: 'If I marry at all, he will be.'

Some men get what they deserve – others remain bachelors.

'Have you set a date for your wedding?' asked Eve.

'No, so far we can't agree on a time,' replied Ruby.

'What's the problem?'

'Well, I won't marry Jim when he's drunk, and he won't marry me when he's sober,' answered Ruby.

'I had very bad luck with both my wives,' confided Leslie to a friend in the pub.

'Is that so? What happened?' enquired his fellow drinker.

'Well,' answered Leslie. 'My first wife ran away with another man and my second wife didn't.'

Harry and Maud had been married thirty-five years when Harry died and left her over £300,000. However, after a year the estate still hadn't been settled and Maud was fed up with all the legal red tape.

'Sometimes,' she confided to her friend Madge, 'I'm sorry Harry ever died. Do you know I'd give £10,000 of that money to have him back again.'

Basil and Carol had decided to elope so they made their plans with great care and secrecy. On the appointed night, Basil quietly placed the ladder against the window-sill of Carol's bedroom, holding the ladder at the bottom. As Carol climbed on to the ladder she rattled it.

'Hush,' whispered Basil. 'We don't want to make a noise or we'll have your father up.'

'He's already up,' replied Carol. 'He's holding the top of the ladder.'

The young actor dashed into the house and, grabbing his father by the arm, shouted in excitement: 'Dad, I've got a wonderful part in a David Puttnam film. It will really test my acting ability as I have to play the part of a man who has been married for twenty-five years.'

'That's wonderful, son, wonderful,' encouraged the father. 'Keep trying and some day you may get a speaking part.'

One night, a great flash of lightning caused a gas explosion and blew Sid and Violet fifty feet into the air in their double bed. Violet was not the least bit upset: she said it was the first time in twenty years that she and Sid had been out together.

Her wedding day was approaching and all the arrangements were made but the bride-to-be was worried that all would not go well.

'You know,' she said to her mother, 'the whole thing could be ruined if we overlooked some insignificant little detail.'

'Don't worry,' her mother assured her, 'I'll make sure he gets there.'

The lawyer asked Mr Dennis to call at his office to discuss the contents of his will.

'What appears to be the problem?' asked Mr Dennis.

'I think you made an error in the draft you left me,' said the lawyer in his most professional manner.

'What is that?' probed Mr Dennis.

'In this draft, you leave your wife £20,000 a year so long as she remains unmarried, and £50,000 if she marries again,' pointed out the lawyer.

'That's right,' affirmed Mr Dennis. 'The poor bugger who marries her deserves it!'

It was near the end of the honeymoon which had been spent in an isolated cottage in Scotland. The honeymooners had explored the surrounding area, walked the gorselands and, in the evenings, sat at the log fire in the cottage. They were without radio, television, tapes, newspapers and contact with the outside world. Just the two of them and the rugged wilderness.

'Wouldn't it be nice to see a friend?' said the wife on the eve of their departure.

'Yes,' said the husband with a sigh, 'or even an enemy.'

'It's appalling, absolutely appalling,' fired Mrs Morris, lowering her newspaper.

'What is?' enquired her husband.

'I've just read that in some parts of Africa a wife can be bought for £10!'

'Well,' shrugged her husband. 'I suppose there are profiteers there just as in other countries.'

'The man who gives in when he is wrong is a wise man,' said the minister from the pulpit, 'but he who gives in when he is right is . . .'

'Married,' interrupted a voice from the congregation.

The honeymoon is over when he stops helping with the dishes – and does them himself.

It was the first night of their honeymoon and they made love. Then the bride wanted to make love again . . . and again . . . and again . . . and again. Finally, she rolled over and went into a deep sleep.

The groom, exhausted, tumbled from the bed, put on his pyjamas and staggered into the bathroom. As he stood at the toilet nothing happened so he opened his pyjamas a little more – still nothing. Eventually, he poked around inside and said. 'It's all right, you can come out now, she's asleep.'

Ken came home from work one night to find his wife terribly upset.

'What's the matter, darling?' he asked as he put his arm around her.

'I cooked you a special dinner and the dog has eaten it,' she sobbed.

'Not to worry, my sweet,' said Ken in a comforting tone. 'I'll buy you another dog.'

After the death of her husband, Margaret went to a medium who made contact with him.

'Are you happy, Sam?' asked Margaret.

'Yes,' replied Sam. 'Very happy.'

'Happier than you were when you were with me?' enquired Margaret.

'Yes, indeed,' answered Sam. 'I'm much happier here than I was when I was with you.'

'Isn't that wonderful,' said Margaret wistfully. 'Heaven must be a lovely place.'

'Who said anything about heaven?' questioned Sam.

'You're charged with pushing your mother-in-law out of a window in your tenth floor apartment,' announced the judge to the mild-looking little man standing facing him.

'Yes, sir,' replied the little man, 'but I did it on the spur of the moment. I did it without thinking.'

'That may be so,' lectured the judge. 'But don't you see how very dangerous it might have been for anyone walking underneath at the time?'

Amanda Dunn's third divorce was final and she was celebrating with her friend, Dora.

'You know, Dora,' said the new divorcee, 'I was married three times but I'm still a virgin.'

'That's difficult to believe,' countered Dora. 'Three husbands and you're still a virgin. How could that possibly happen?'

'Simple,' replied Amanda sipping her drink. 'My first husband was a politician and all he wanted to do was to talk to it.'

'And your second husband?'

'He was an optician and all he wanted was to look at it.'

'What about your third husband?' asked Dora.

'Oh, he was a food critic!'

The minister was standing outside the church saying his farewells and giving his blessing to the members of the congregation as they left. Suddenly he was hustled to one side by Mrs Dexter.

'You will have to do something about my husband,' gritted Mrs Dexter. 'He has gone and changed his will.'

'Be calm, Mrs Dexter, be calm,' urged the minister. 'Perhaps we should talk about it.'

'There's no talking to be done,' retorted Mrs Dexter. 'Just tell my husband to change his will back to what it was.'

'I think, Mrs Dexter, this is more a matter for a solicitor. It really does not appear to be a religious matter,' said the minister.

'Of course it's a religious matter!' shouted Mrs Dexter. 'He has joined a religious community which believes in reincarnation and now he's leaving everything to himself!'

In the week before her wedding a young bride was very nervous in case she made a mistake at the ceremony. The minister tried to put her fears at rest by pointing out the service was very simple.

'If it will help you,' said the minister, 'just remember when you enter the church you walk up the aisle. The groom and best man will be waiting before the alter. Then the congregation will sing a hymn. So the order is aisle, alter, hymn. Aisle, alter, hymn. Remember that and you can't go wrong.'

However, on the wedding day, the minister was horrified to hear the bride saying as she walked towards him, 'I'll alter him!'

After reading an advertisement of the effects of a particular brand of vitamin tablets, a woman sent for a supply. After finishing the prescribed course, she was so pleased with the results she took time to write to the manufacturers. 'Since taking your tablets I am a different woman,' she wrote. 'My husband is delighted.'

The girl had been married two weeks when her mother-in-law called to see her or, as the girl thought, to see that her son was being well treated.

'How is married life?' asked the mother-in-law as she beady-eyed the kitchen.

'Quite frankly,' replied the girl, 'it's not as I thought it would be.'

'Oh, and how is that?' asked dragon lady.

'Well, for one thing, your son never stops grumbling,' pointed out the girl.

'After all, dear, you did marry him for better or worse,' came the acid reply.

'Yes, and I seem to have got him for worse!'

'My husband went to a mindreader and he only charged him half price as there was so little to read.'

'I suppose if I died you'd marry again in a very short time,' shouted the wife at her husband.

'Whatever makes you say that?' said her husband, as he practised putting with his umbrella.

'Oh, I know you. You'd probably give her all my jewellery,' went on the wife.

'Don't be silly,' remarked the husband, as he changed his grip on the umbrella.

'I'm not being silly,' stormed the wife. 'She would probably get my car as well.'

'Such nonsense,' claimed the husband, as he changed his stance.

'And my golf clubs,' flared the wife. 'You would probably give her my golf clubs.'

'Definitely not,' retorted the husband. 'She's left-handed!'

Percy Knott was a very shy young man who loved Rosemary very much and wanted to marry her but never had enough courage to ask. One day, he had a rush of blood to the head and decided to propose so he telephoned her.

'Hello,' answered a soft, sweet, female voice.

'Hello, is that Rosemary?' enquired Percy.

'Yes. Rosemary speaking.'

'Rosemary, darling, will you marry me?'

'Of course I will. Who's speaking?'

A business man arrived home at eight in the morning and told his wife he had been up late at a meeting with the union. When the meeting ended, he drove his secretary home, she made him some coffee and, considering the late hour, suggested he stay at her place, which he did.

His wife listened to his explanation with a frown, eagle-eyed him then shouted: 'Don't you lie to me. I know what you were doing. You were playing cards at the club with those no-good friends of yours!'

'Sarah, I'm very worried about my husband.'
   'Why, what's the matter?' asked Sarah.
'He spends a lot of time talking to flowers.'
'I wouldn't worry about that. A lot of people talk to flowers.'
'When they're a design in the wallpaper?'

Joan went to a fortune teller who spread a number of cards on the table then said in a slow and deliberate tone. 'You will soon meet a tall, dark handsome man with whom you will fall madly in love.'
   'Will he love me?' asked Joan.
   'He will love you very deeply and will give you many gifts,' intoned the fortune teller.
   'Is he rich?' enquired the interested Joan.
   The fortune teller added more cards to those on the table and nodded. 'Very, very, rich. I can also see water so you will travel far with him, probably around the world.'
   'May I ask another question?'
   'Of course.'
   'How do I get rid of my husband?'

The man was explaining to the police officer how he had awakened to find his wife pouring petrol over him.
   'What,' asked the police officer as he made some notes in his notebook, 'do you think she was planning to do?'

'Frankly, officer,' answered the husband, 'I think she was trying to make a fuel out of me.'

'My husband,' observed Elizabeth, 'is of the Beat generation – dead Beat!'

Husband: 'Shall we go and see a film?'
Wife: 'I didn't get all dressed up to go and sit in the cinema.'
Husband: 'We'll go visiting then.'
Wife: 'Nor did I get all dressed up to go and sit in someone else's house.'
Husband: 'Well, what about a night club?'
Wife: 'I'm not dressed.'

The young wife questioned her handsome husband about his two earlier marriages. 'What happened to your previous wives?'

'My first wife died of mushroom poisoning,' answered the husband.

'And your second wife?' she asked.

'Oh, she died of a fractured skull,' her husband shrugged. 'It was her own bloody fault – she wouldn't eat the mushrooms!'

Two brothers, both actors, received the news that their father was critically ill in a London hospital as the result of a car accident. The condition of their father was so grave they were requested to get to the hospital as soon as possible.

One brother, who was appearing in London, reached the hospital quickly. However, the other brother, who was on tour, took longer. When he reached the hospital he ran up the steps and ran along the corridor only to be met by his brother who told him their father was dead.

The late arrival was greatly distressed and cried, 'I never even got a chance to see him. What were his last words?'

'He had no last words,' replied the other brother putting a comforting arm around him. 'Mother was with him to the end.'

'My marriage was a marriage of convenience,' confessed Barbara. 'I met my husband in the ladies' toilet when he walked in by mistake.'

'If my mother-in-law lived in India she would be considered sacred,' remarked Ted as he sipped his beer.

'I got a beautiful dog for my husband.'
'Boy, that was good swop!'

A married man arrived home very late and told his wife he had been working at the office. She was already in bed and watched her husband as he undressed to join her.

'Edward,' she suddenly screamed. 'Where are your shorts?'
'Christ!' exclaimed the husband. 'I've been robbed!'

It was the Sunday before Christmas and Mrs Twig was in her kitchen when she heard the band of the Salvation Army playing a Christmas selection. She went into the lounge to tell her husband only to find him sprawled in an armchair, unwashed, unshaven, untidy and snoring loudly. Shaking her head sadly, she responded to the ringing of the door bell to find a trim young girl in the uniform of the Salvation Army standing on the step.

'Good afternoon,' said the girl. 'It's our Christmas collection for the needy and I wonder if you would care to contribute?'

'Certainly,' said Mrs Twig and gave very generously.

'Thank you very much,' acknowledged the girl. 'Would you like a hymn?'

'Yes,' said Mrs Twig wearily. 'How about him with the big drum?'

'The man who marries my daughter will be getting a great prize,' boasted the proud father.

'Is that so, sir?' asked Angus. 'Could I have a wee look at it first?'

A man walked into the doctor's surgery and said. 'It's my wife, doctor. She can't speak, she's lost her voice completely. I'm very worried about her.'

'Nothing to worry about,' assured the doctor. 'She's probably the victim of this little bug that's going around. Nothing dangerous, just inconvenient. An injection has an immediate effect and she'll be talking right away.'

'Is that so, doctor?' mused the man. 'Nothing to worry about, eh? So if I bring her to see you in a couple of months you'll give her an injection?'

'Percy and I have been married ten years and never had a quarrel,' said Margaret to Edwina as they shopped together. 'If a difference of opinion arises and I am right, Percy always gives in immediately.'

'And if he is right?' queried Edwina.

'That never occurs,' replied Margaret.

'Darling, Mrs Smith next door has a coat exactly the same as mine,' said Mrs Briggs.

'Ah,' said her husband with a smile. 'I suppose that's a hint that you want a new coat?'

'Well, it would be a lot cheaper than moving to a new house,' replied his wife.

'I say, old man, has your wife ever been abroad?'

'Certainly not! She has always been a very respectable lady.'

'Frankly, I owe everything I have to my husband – indigestion, headaches, worn hands, bad back, sore feet – the lot.'

Mrs Mills suspected that her husband, a successful businessman, was having an affair with his secretary.

She went to a solicitor who specialized in marital cases. Immediately, he put a private investigator to work and within a week the solicitor had enough information to confirm the wife's suspicions.

'You are quite right, Mrs Mills,' advised the solicitor. 'Your husband and his secretary are lovers.'

'I'll get him!' exploded Mrs Mills. 'I'll make him sorry he ever looked at another woman. How much would it cost to get enough evidence to sue him for every penny he has?'

'With one investigator, a photographer, a witness and my fees,' muttered the solicitor, 'I would say about £3000.'

'Get started right away,' ordered Mrs Mills. 'I can get that amount of money from my boyfriend!'

The police inspector viewed the dead body of the man lying on the floor of the bedroom.

'Tell me,' said the police inspector to the wife. 'Why did you shoot your husband with a bow and arrow?'

'I didn't want to waken the children,' explained the wife.

The visitor was admiring a magnificent stuffed bear in an ancestral home of an English lord. 'What a wonderful specimen,' he said. 'Where did you bag him?'

'Northern Canada, on a hunting trip with my husband,' replied her ladyship.

'What's he stuffed with?' asked the visitor.

'My husband,' replied the lady.

A man entered a well-known chain store and asked an assistant to select a gift for his wife.

'What do you want?' asked the assistant.

'Oh, anything at all,' replied the man.

'Well, what do you think your wife would like? A skirt? A twin set?' probed the helpful girl.

'A twin set sounds good, what is it?' said the customer.

'This, sir, is a twin set,' said the girl holding up the clothes.

'That'll be fine,' nodded the man.

'What size and colour?' enquired the girl.

'About the size of that lady,' replied the man indicating a woman standing at another counter, 'and any colour will do. By the way, instead of putting it in a plastic bag, could you wrap it for me?'

'Is it a surprise present for your wife?' smiled the girl.

'It certainly is. She's expecting a pearl necklace!'

The speaker had just told the audience that her organization was sending condoms worth £2,000,000 to India in an effort to stem the birth rate.

'I say,' one man shouted, 'couldn't they just do what my wife does – pretend they're asleep?'

A British commoner was marrying a foreign princess and was being briefed on the protocol of the procedure of the marriage.

'When you go to the bridal suite you must not make any advance,' the official told the commoner. 'The princess will offer you her honour and you will honour her offer.'

And so it was all night – honour, offer, honour, offer, honour, offer . . .

'You seem to have a very good marriage, Fred,' observed Wilf. 'You've been married for twenty-five years and still going strong. What's the secret?'

'No secret, Wilf,' replied Fred. 'There are two good reasons why my marriage has lasted. First, my wife and I go out every weekend. Second, she doesn't ask me where I go and I don't ask her where she goes.'

A seventy-five-year-old man married an eighteen-year-old girl. After only a month of marriage she caught him with a sixty-year-old woman.

'What's she got that I haven't?' stormed the young wife.

'Patience,' her husband replied.

The husband excitedly charged into his house and gleefully told his wife, 'I've found this great job – good salary, company car, paid statutory holidays, flexi hours and six weeks leave a year.'

'That's wonderful, darling,' cheered his wife.

'Yes, I knew you'd be pleased,' gushed her husband. 'You start on Monday.'

'Darling,' he whispered, as they lay in bed on the first night of their honeymoon, 'just think for the rest of your life you will have to put up with this ugly face of mine.'

'Not to worry,' the bride sweetly replied. 'You'll be out at work all day.'

The husband, feeling rather passionate, jumped into bed beside his wife. He was prepared for some lovemaking but before he got started his wife began to complain about the cost of living.

'Everything is going up,' she whined. 'The price of food, the cost of clothes, the beauty shop, even the little things you need around the house like cleaning materials. I'd be happy if just one thing went down.'

'You just got your wish,' came the sleepy reply.

It was at a New Year's party and the husband toasted his wife by raising his glass and saying. 'Well, darling, I wish you all that you wish me.'

'What are you trying to do?' snarled his wife. 'Start a row.'

'Will you love me when I'm old and wrinkled?' asked the wife coyly as she admired the gift her husband had just given her for their tenth wedding anniversary.

'Of course I do, darling,' replied her husband from behind the morning paper.

Doctor: 'Did you sleep with your wife last night?'
Husband: 'Not a wink.'

Hilda Hatch had been talking for a long time to the doctor about her husband's symptoms. 'I'm afraid, doctor,' she said finally, 'that my husband has some terrible mental affliction. Sometimes I talk to him for hours then discover he hasn't heard a single word.'

'That's not an affliction,' was the weary reply, 'that's a gift.'

A university in Ulster recently carried out a survey of how married women rated their leisure time. Sex came in a poor fourth, lagging behind watching television, reading and knitting. And though many of the married women stated they enjoyed sex, some indicated they enjoyed it more while watching television, reading or knitting.

The hotel porter took the couple to their room and was given a generous tip.

'Thank you, sir,' he said. 'Will there be anything else?'
'No, thank you,' replied the man.

'Anything for your wife, sir?' enquired the porter.

The man thought for a moment then said, 'Yes, bring me a nice postcard to send her.'

'Why did you never marry?' asked one man.

'Well,' replied the other, 'why buy a book when you can join a lending library?'

'Ronald's wife is very beautiful,' said the first man.

'Yes, indeed,' agreed his colleague. 'A bit like Venus de Milo.'

'Venus de Milo?'

'Yes, beautiful but not all there.'

A world famous and much-married Hollywood film actress was asked by a television interviewer how many husbands she had had. A little puzzled, she replied, 'You mean apart from my own?'

A woman was applying for a maintenance order against her husband who had not made provision for her or her seven children.

'He deserted me seven years ago,' she answered in reply to the solicitor's question.

'But,' said the solicitor, 'if your husband deserted you seven years ago, how come three of your children are aged two, four and six?'

'Well, you see,' said the woman, 'he keeps coming back to apologize.'

It was at the peak of a row and the wife shrieked at her husband. 'If only I had taken my mother's advice, I never would have married you.'

'What? Do you mean to tell me your mother tried to stop you from marrying me?' shouted the husband.

'She most certainly did. She did everything in her power to stop the marriage.'

'Oh,' sighed the husband, raising his hands to his head. 'How I've wronged that woman.'

I had everything a man could want,' sobbed the husband. 'Money, a lovely home, the love of a beautiful and wealthy woman. Then, one day, my wife walked in!'

Tony was sitting in the pub staring sadly at his drink when he was joined by Richard.

'What's the matter, Tony?' said Richard. 'You look really worried.'

'I'm going to be a father,' muttered Tony.

'Oh, and what's the problem?' asked Richard. 'Is your wife not happy about the forthcoming event?'

'That's the problem,' confided Tony. 'She doesn't know yet.'

'You know,' grumbled the man as he drank his beer and puffed on his pipe, 'marriage isn't what it used to be.'

'In what way?' asked his young male drinking friend as he sipped his white wine.

'Years ago,' said the pipe smoker, 'when you got married, a woman cooked for you, cleaned for you, sewed for you and cared for you. Today when a woman says "I do", it's the last bloody thing she does for you.'

The telephone shrilled on the bedside table and the husband eventually fumbled it to his ear and yawned, 'Yes'.

After listening for a moment, he stumbled out of bed and began dressing.

'Where are you going?' asked his wife.

'A gorilla from the zoo has escaped and is believed to be in this area and the police have asked the men around here to form a search party,' replied her husband.

'An escaped gorilla!' yelled his wife. 'Surely you're not going to leave me alone. What am I supposed to do if he comes in here and jumps on me?'

'Same as you do with me,' grunted her husband. 'Tell him you've got a headache!'

'Did you get my cheque for a thousand kisses?' asked a man when he telephoned his wife who was on holiday.

'Yes, indeed,' gushed the wife, 'and the manager of the hotel cashed it!'

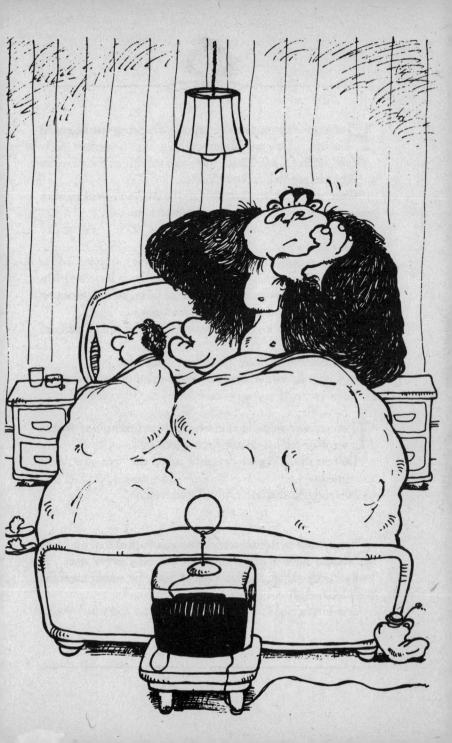

'Haven't seen you for some time,' Charles greeted Len. 'Is it true you're now divorced?'

'Yes,' replied Len. 'Quite true.'

'What happened?' asked Charles.

'Well, one morning, I dressed in the dark and went to work wearing the postman's trousers,' sighed Len.

The new secretary was a very attractive, sexy girl so, at the first opportunity, the boss said, 'If you have no plans for the weekend, why don't you come down to my little cottage by the sea and we'll have some fun?'

'That would be lovely,' replied the girl. 'And I'll bring my boyfriend.'

'Your boyfriend? Why bring him?' asked the boss.

'In case your wife wants some fun too,' announced the girl.

The seventy-year-old man who had married a girl of twenty went to see his doctor for a check-up.

'Do you think I'm overweight?' asked the man after being examined.

'No,' replied the doctor, 'just overmatched.'

Sammy was of the old school and maintained that husbands should have a night out with the boys every week. So every Friday night, regular as clockwork, he would meet the boys for their night out.

One Friday night, he didn't return home and was away for

three years. Then on a Friday afternoon he returned as suddenly as he had disappeared.

His wife was delighted and said, 'I must telephone our friends and invite them over to celebrate your return.'

'Invite them over when?' asked Sammy.

'Tonight of course,' responded his wife.

'Oh, no, not tonight,' growled Sammy. 'This is my night out.'

T he two men were having a business lunch when two women entered the restaurant. 'Christ!' exclaimed one. 'My wife and my mistress have just walked in.'

'My words exactly,' remarked the other man.

'S ometimes I worry about my husband, doctor. He does very weird things,' said Mrs Jones in a worried voice.

'Why, what has he done now?' asked the doctor.

'Well, he watered the lawn with beer so it will come up half cut,' replied the weary Mrs Jones.

A doctor and his wife were out for a seaside walk and a very vivacious young blonde waved to the doctor.

'Who was that?' asked his wife.

'Oh, just a young woman I met professionally,' explained the doctor in a casual manner.

'Professionally, eh?' murmured his wife. 'Yours or hers?'

'My husband is very kind to animals,' said Mrs Temple. 'My husband contributes to sick animal charities,' declared Mrs Scott. 'Unfortunately, he doesn't know they are sick when he bets on them.'

Then there was the Jewish couple, saddened when told by a teacher that she had to chastise their son for playing with his genitals.

'That is a very sad thing to hear,' observed the wife. 'Some of my best friends are genitals.'

The old married couple arrived at the hotel only to be told by the receptionist there was nothing available except the bridal suite.

'But we've been married forty-five years,' argued the husband.

'So?' snapped the receptionist. 'I can let you have the ball-room – but you don't have to dance!'

The hard-working husband went on a two week sales promotion trip covering most of the country. All the time his thoughts were on one thing – getting back to his wife. He never looked at or thought about another woman. At last, the business trip was over and he rushed home to hold his wife in his arms.

As he went into the house he saw his wife sitting in an armchair watching television.

'I'm back, darling,' he called. 'Did you miss me while I was away?'

'Oh,' said the wife, still watching television. 'Have you been away?'

The vicar was standing outside the church on a Sunday morning speaking to the parishioners as they left.

'Good morning, Mr Jones,' the vicar greeted the man.

'Morning, vicar,' said Mr Jones. 'I enjoyed your sermon today.'

'I'm so glad,' beamed the vicar.

'In it you said it was wrong for anyone to profit from the mistakes of others. Is that correct?' questioned Mr Jones.

'Quite correct, Mr Jones, quite correct,' agreed the vicar.

'In that case, will you consider refunding the fee I paid you for marrying me to Gwen six years ago?'

'I'm worried about my wife,' said Brown. 'She drives like lightning.'

'You mean she drives very fast?' asked Ross.

'No, she's always striking trees,' replied Brown.

Donna walked into the bedroom wearing sexy black under-wear which caused her husband to whistle.

'Why the whistle?' asked Donna. 'It's the same old package you saw last night, only the wrapping has been changed.'

'My husband is an efficiency expert in a large firm,' said the first wife.

'What does an efficiency expert do?' asked the second wife.

'Well, if women did it, they'd call it nagging,' said the first wife.

As the woman was having her fortune told the fortune teller frowned as she studied the cards. 'Prepare yourself for widowhood,' she whispered. 'Your husband will soon die a violent death.'

'Now, tell me,' questioned the woman, 'will I be acquitted?'

The married couple went to see the doctor who examined the cuts, bruises and hacks on the husband's leg and then remarked. 'That was a pretty rough game you were playing. What was it, football, hockey or rugby?'

'Bridge,' answered the husband quietly.

Marriage is a process by which a man finds out what sort of husband his wife thinks she should have had.

The man went into a butcher's shop and asked for a large duck.

'I'm sorry,' apologised the butcher, 'but we have no ducks today. How about a nice leg of lamb?'

'Don't be daft,' grumbled the customer. 'How can I tell my wife I shot a leg of lamb?'

There's nothing I wouldn't do for my wife,' said Denis as he drank his whisky. 'And there's nothing she wouldn't do for me. And that's how we go through life – doing nothing for each other.'

The husband was sneaking into the house at 4 a.m. when he was confronted by his wife in the hall. 'So,' she shouted, 'home is the best place after all!'

'I don't know about that,' gurgled her husband, 'but it's the only place that's open.'

Why did you divorce your wife?'
'The parrot kept saying "Kiss me, Tom".'
'That doesn't seem much of a reason.'
'My name happens to be Richard.'

Before I married you,' declared the woman, 'I could have been a model. I was asked to pose for a painting.'
'Really?' said her disinterested husband.
'Yes, a well-known artist was doing a painting of Eve and

the Serpent and he wanted me to pose for him,' answered the wife.

'Oh, and who was to be Eve?'

S imon was sitting admiring a bracelet he had bought for his wife as a present for their tenth wedding anniversary.

'That's a lovely gift,' observed his friend, Mark. 'I'm sure she'll be very pleased.'

'You know, Mark,' confided Simon, 'I never slept with my wife before we were married. Did you?'

'I don't really know,' replied Mark thoughtfully. 'What was her maiden name?'

T he small girl viewed the pregnant figure of her mother then asked. 'Mummy, why is your tummy like that?'

'That's a baby,' replied her mother.

'A baby?' questioned the little girl.

'Yes, darling, a baby.'

'Who gave it to you?' continued the little girl.

'Daddy gave it to me,' answered the mother.

The child was silent for a moment then went into another room to see her father.

'Daddy, you know that baby you gave to Mummy?'

'Yes, darling,' responded her father.

'Well, she's swallowed it.'

The couple went to a bottle party and, as the husband was talking to the host, he mentioned his wife had brought a bottle of wine. As he spoke he spotted his wife and waved to her by making a sign of a bottle being poured.

His wife replied by putting her hand on her left breast and then touching her bottom.

'Dammit!' exclaimed the husband.

'Something wrong?' asked the host.

'My wife says she left it behind,' replied the husband.

'We mustn't have any more children,' said the wife with great determination.

'Oh,' said the husband, 'that surprises me. You always said you wanted a fourth child.'

'Well, I've changed my mind,' replied the wife. 'I've just seen a programme on television on world population and the narrator said every fourth child born was Chinese.'

The father was putting his young daughter to bed when she said. 'Daddy, will you lift me into bed the way you lift Mummy?'

So he lifted her into bed.

'Daddy, will you fluff my pillows the way you fluff Mummy's pillows?'

So he fluffed her pillows.

'Daddy, will you tuck me in the way you do with Mummy?'

So he tucked her in.

'Daddy, will you whisper in my ear the way you do with Mummy?'

So he whispered 'Goodnight' in her ear to which the child replied, 'Not tonight, Teddy, I've got a headache.'

'It wasn't until my wife left me I realized my loss,' said the man glumly.

'You miss her?' asked a friend.

'Yes, and my cheque book, my car, my credit cards and my wallet.'

'Hello, Mrs Benn,' greeted Mrs Dell when they met in a shopping centre. 'I just saw your husband and I must say he looks ever so worried.'

'Oh, hello, Mrs Dell,' replied Mrs Benn. 'My husband saw the doctor this morning and got some bad news.'

'Oh, I'm sorry to hear that. What did the doctor say?' asked Mrs Dell.

'He said my husband was fit for work and then signed him off.'

'Alma,' said the mother to her teenage daughter, 'I think it's about time we had a talk about sex.'

'Sure, mum,' replied Alma. 'What do you want to know?'

Mrs Green was feeling very depressed and went to see her doctor who examined her and then asked a number of questions, including how often she had sex.

'Is it serious, doctor?' the worried woman asked.

'Frankly, Mrs Green, you're suffering from frustration. You need an outlet for your pent-up feelings,' replied the doctor. 'In view of what you've told me about your sex life I recommend you should have sex about four times a week and that should release your tension.'

Mrs Green returned home and told her husband what the doctor had prescribed.

'Right,' said her husband after a long and thoughtful pause, 'put me down for Tuesdays and Saturdays.'

'Your husband has good grounds for divorce, Mrs Fisher,' pointed out the solicitor. 'After all, you deceived him.'

'Nothing of the sort,' retorted Mrs Fisher. 'He deceived me.'

'How did he deceive you?' enquired the solicitor.

'Well, he said he was going out of town and he didn't,' stated Mrs Fisher.

The chief fire officer met one of his young officers who was about to be married. 'I'd like to congratulate you,' said the chief. 'You will always look back on today as the happiest day of your life.'

'Thank you, sir,' replied the young officer, 'but it's tomorrow I'm getting married.'

'Yes,' replied the chief thoughtfully, 'I know.'

Bill had always wanted to search for treasure but never got the opportunity. As a compromise his wife, Sue, bought him a metal detector and they travelled to the north-west coast of Ireland where the Spanish Armada had perished in 1588. The plan was for Bill to search the shoreline with his detector and locate some of the treasure washed up from the wrecks.

One day, Bill and his wife were searching when they came across a little fellow wearing a green suit and hat lying in some gorse.

'Hello,' said Bill. 'Are you a leprechaun?'

'Indeed, I am,' replied the little fellow. 'Indeed, I am.'

'Well, perhaps you could grant me a wish to find some treasure,' suggested Bill.

'I'm sure I could but you must give up something in return. If you let me have your wife in the gorse for an hour I'll tell you where to find some treasure,' said the little fellow.

After a discussion with his wife, Bill agreed.

The little fellow took Sue deeper into the gorse and after an hour of pleasure he asked, 'How old is your husband?'

'Forty,' answered Sue.

'And he still believes in leprechauns?'

The old farmer was standing looking over his farm-yard when he was joined by his wife who linked her arm tightly through his and stood in silence for a moment.

'You know, John,' said the wife, 'come Saturday we'll have been married forty years.'

'Indeed, we will, Martha, indeed, we will,' answered her husband.

'And I was thinking, John, of having a few friends for dinner. We could kill a turkey.'

'Ah now, Martha, why should we punish a turkey for something that happened forty years ago,' replied John softly.

The husband came home from work to find his wife in bed with a neighbour. 'I suppose,' he shouted, glaring at his wife, 'this means my dinner is going to be late again!'

Bank manager: 'What's your husband's average income?'
Wife: 'Between 3 and 4 a.m.'

The police patrol car drew level with a male motorist and the police officer frantically waved him on to the hard shoulder of the motorway. The police officer jumped out of the car and shouted. 'Your wife fell out of your car at the last slip road.'

'Thank God it's only that,' replied the motorist. 'I thought I'd suddenly gone stone deaf.'

Graham came home very late one night. As he slipped into bed his wife sleepily said, 'Is that you, Graham?'
'It bloody well better be,' answered Graham grimly.

'Where are you going on holiday?' asked Leslie.
'We're going to India,' answered Ron.
'Aren't you afraid the hot climate in India might disagree with your wife?' pointed out Leslie.
'It wouldn't dare,' came the grim reply.

'I'm just reading that scientists claim the average person speaks 10,000 words a day,' said Mrs Cree, lowering her newspaper.
'Ah, yes, dear,' observed her husband, 'but remember you are well above average.'

Mrs Bell shook her husband awake from his slumber in the armchair.
'Whatismatter?' mumbled Mr Bell.
'Will you help me straighten up the house?' asked his wife.
'Why?' yawned her husband. 'Is it tilted?'

Cecil had reached retirement and was a very worried man. Most of his life he had enjoyed to the full but he lived for the day and hadn't saved, so his financial position was not good.
'I don't know what we're going to do, Joan,' he moaned to

his wife. 'I'm being forced to retire but really we can't afford it. I'll have to try and find another job.'

'Don't worry, darling,' said his wife handing him a bank-book, 'we have enough in that to give us a comfortable life.'

'That's great,' cried Cecil in amazement. 'I didn't know you had this account, how did you do it?'

'Well,' said his wife shyly, 'every time you made love to me during our married life I put some money into the bank.'

'Wonderful! Wonderful!' shouted the overjoyed husband. 'But why didn't you tell me before? If I'd known about this account I'd have given you all my business.'

'My wife and I had a bit of a row, last night,' said Walter to his friend as they drove to work. 'She wanted to go to the opera and I wanted to see a film. But we soon sorted it out.'

'And did you enjoy the opera?' asked his friend.

The woman was stopped in the street by a researcher. 'We're doing a survey on marriage,' he said. 'Are you happily married?'

'I suppose so,' replied the woman.

'Have you a lot in common with your husband?' the researcher asked.

'No, not really,' came the reply.

'Have you anything in common with your husband?' the researcher persisted.

'Well, we were both married on the same day,' nodded the woman.

'You know,' complained Mrs Rooney to her husband, 'when you come home from work I ask you about your day, how things went, what you did and all that. But you never ask me about my day. Here I am with five children to look after, the house to clean, the washing to do and all the shopping to get and never a word of interest from you.'

'Well, then,' said Mr Rooney. 'How was your day?'

'Don't ask,' moaned Mrs Rooney, raising her hands in despair. 'Just don't ask.'

'George,' said May, 'I think our dog is getting old.'

'What makes you think that?' asked her husband.

'He seems to be going a bit deaf,' replied May.

'Nonsense,' said George. 'Not a thing wrong with him. Look, I'll show you. Rover! Sit!'

'Well?' said May.

'You're quite right, dear. I'll get the shovel and clean it up.'

An octogenarian was being interviewed on his sixty years of marriage. 'Is there one big difference between your marriage today and when you were first married?' asked the interviewer.

'Well,' said the man after pondering for a moment. 'It now takes me all night to do what I used to do all night.'

'Surely you don't believe your husband's story about going fishing,' stirred the acid-tongued neighbour. 'I noticed he didn't bring any fish back.'

'That's what makes me believe he was fishing,' replied the wife.

The young bride was telling her mother how wonderful marriage was. 'Do you know, Mummy,' she said, 'Tony gives me everything I ask for.'

'Which merely shows,' replied her mother grimly, 'that you are not asking for enough.'

The woman studied the crystal ball and said to the man, 'I see a buried treasure.'

'Yes,' said the man wearily. 'Probably my wife's first husband.'

'How's the new car going, Bill?'
'Fine, only it costs a lot to keep.'
'And how's your wife?'
'Just the same, thank you.'

'Well, darling,' asked the eager wife. 'How did Mr Lee act when you asked him for an increase in salary?'
'He was like a lamb,' replied her husband.
'What did he say?'
'Bah.'

'What are you looking for?' demanded the wife.
'Nothing,' replied her husband.
'You'll find it in the bottle where the whisky was,' came the sharp reply.

Wife: 'I had to marry you to find out how stupid you are.'
Husband: 'You should have known that the minute I asked you to marry me.'

'I've been travelling backwards for three hours,' moaned Charlie to his wife as he got off the train. 'And you know how much I hate that.'
'Why,' enquired his wife, 'didn't you ask the person sitting opposite to change seats with you?'
'I couldn't,' complained Charlie. 'There wasn't anyone there.'

'But my dear,' protested the henpecked husband, 'I've done nothing. You've been talking for two hours and I haven't said a word.'
'I know,' replied his acid-faced wife. 'But you listen like a real smart arse!'

A man arrived home from work and was appalled to see his wife's car in the lounge.
'How the hell did you get your car in there?' stormed the husband.

'Nothing to it,' replied the wife nonchalantly. 'When I got to the kitchen I turned right!'

'K nickers,' remarked the husband as he watched his wife dressing, 'are not the best thing in the world.'
'No, but they're next to it,' replied his wife.

☐	WORLD'S BEST AFTER-DINNER JOKES Edward Phillips	0-00-637960-5	£2.99
☐	WORLD'S BEST SKIING JOKES Ernest Forbes	0-00-638246-0	£2.99
☐	WORLD'S BEST MOTORING JOKES Edward Phillips	0-00-638265-7	£2.99
☐	WORLD'S BEST BOSS JOKES Edward Phillips	0-00-638241-X	£2.99
☐	WORLD'S BEST DRINKING JOKES Ernest Forbes	0-00-638242-8	£2.99
☐	WORLD'S BEST DIRTY JOKES Mr J	0-00-637784-X	£2.99

These books are available from your local bookseller or can be ordered direct from the publishers.

To order direct just tick the titles you want and fill in the form below:

Name:

Address:

Postcode:

Send to: HarperCollins Mail Order, Dept 8, HarperCollins*Publishers*, Westerhill Road, Bishopbriggs, Glasgow G64 2QT.

Please enclose a cheque or postal order or your authority to debit your Visa/Access account –

Credit card no:

Expiry date:

Signature:

– to the value of the cover price plus:

UK & BFPO: Add £1.00 for the first and 25p for each additional book ordered.

Overseas orders including Eire, please add £2.95 service charge.

Books will be sent by surface mail but quotes for airmail despatches will be given on request.

24 HOUR TELEPHONE ORDERING SERVICE FOR ACCESS/VISA CARDHOLDERS –

TEL: GLASGOW 041-772 2281 or LONDON 081-307 4052